EDGE BOOKS

Revised and Updated

War Planes

Stealth Attack Fighters

The F-117A Nighthawks

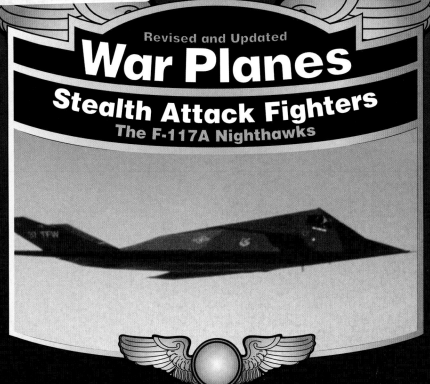

by **Michael and Gladys Green**

Consultant:
Raymond L. Puffer, PhD, Historian
Air Force Flight Test Center
Edwards Air Force Base, California

Capstone
press

Mankato, Minnesota

Edge Books are published by Capstone Press,
151 Good Counsel Drive, P.O. Box 669, Mankato, Minnesota 56002.
www.capstonepress.com

Library of Congress Cataloging-in-Publication Data
Green, Michael, 1952–
    Stealth attack fighters : the F-117A Nighthawks / by Michael and Gladys Green —
Rev. and updated.
        p. cm. — (Edge books. War planes)
    Includes bibliographical references and index.
    ISBN-13: 978-1-4296-1320-0 (hardcover)
    ISBN-10: 1-4296-1320-3 (hardcover)
    1. F-117 (Jet fighter plane) — Juvenile literature. I. Green, Gladys, 1954– II.
Title. III. Series.
UG1242.F5G713 2008
623.74'63 — dc22   2007031336

Summary: Discusses the design and equipment of the stealth attack fighter known as
    the F-117A Nighthawk and its use by the Air Force in military missions.

Editorial Credits
Carrie A. Braulick, editor; Jo Miller, photo researcher; Katy Kudela, revised
    edition editor; Kyle Grenz, revised edition designer

Photo Credits
Defense Visual Information Center (DVIC), 1, 7, 24;
    SSGT Aaron D. Allmon II, USAF, cover
Photo by Ted Carlson/Fotodynamics, 4, 9, 10, 18, 20, 23, 27, 29
Photri-Microstock, 13, 16–17

1 2 3 4 5 6 13 12 11 10 09 08

Table of Contents

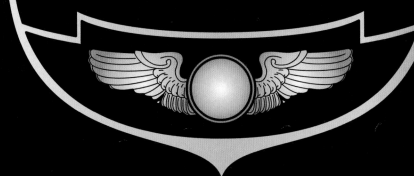

The F-117A in Action

Learn about

- Stealth planes
- F-117A development
- F-117A features

Just after midnight, two U.S. Air Force F-117A Nighthawks fly over an enemy country. On the ground, dozens of radar antennas flood the sky with microwaves. But enemy radar operators still cannot see any sign of a threat on their radar screens.

The F-117A pilots look at cockpit screens to see their targets. Two large bombs drop out of each F-117A.

Moments later, buildings belonging to the enemy government explode. The enemy soldiers fire bullets into the sky, but they cannot see targets on their radar screens. The F-117A pilots safely return to a nearby air base.

Building the F-117A

U.S. Air Force officials became interested in building a stealth plane in the 1940s. Radar-guided guns and missiles had destroyed hundreds of American planes. A stealth plane would be nearly invisible to enemy radar. In the mid-1970s, materials became available for airplane manufacturers to design this type of plane.

In 1978, the Air Force agreed to pay Lockheed Advanced Development Projects to build a stealth fighter. This secret design facility is known as "Skunk Works." The Air Force called the plane the F-117A Stealth Strike Fighter. The company built two test models of the plane.

A group of F-117As is called a spectre of Nighthawks.

In 1982, the Air Force received a final F-117A model. It was the world's first stealth combat aircraft.

Today, the Air Force has more than 40 F-117As in service. All F-117As are located at Holloman Air Force Base in New Mexico.

Stealth Technology

The F-117A's features hide it from enemy radar as pilots fly to their targets. Radar systems send powerful beams of radio energy through the air. After the beams hit a plane, the plane bounces back part of the energy to the radar station. Enemy forces then can see the plane's location on their radar screens.

The F-117A is covered with radar-absorbent material (RAM). The material absorbs the beams to keep them from bouncing back to the station.

EDGE FACT

The Air Force works hard to maintain its Nighthawks. An air bubble in the paint could be enough for a plane to show up on an enemy radar screen.

The F-117A's doors have jagged edges.

Other features prevent radar beams from reaching the station. The F-117A's design causes radar beams to bounce off in several directions. Jagged edges on the F-117A's doors and panels also decrease the reflection of radar beams.

Inside the F-117A

Learn about
- F-117A engines
- Flight controls
- F-117A onboard computer

The F-117A is different from other military planes. Flat panels called facets give the plane a triangular look. The F-117A's windshield is coated with a film that hides the pilot's helmet from enemy radar.

The F-117A has a large, V-shaped tail. This tail controls the aircraft's altitude above the ground. The V-shaped tail also helps pilots turn the plane in the air.

Inside the Cockpit

An F-117A pilot's main cockpit controls are the control stick and the **throttle**. The control stick steers the plane. The throttle controls the speed of the aircraft.

The F-117A's cockpit has other equipment to help pilots perform missions. A head-up display (HUD) is located in front of the pilot. This screen allows the pilot to see flight information without looking down at the cockpit controls. A full-color moving map display helps the pilot keep track of the plane's surroundings.

Onboard Computer

The F-117A is hard to fly. Most planes have curved, sleek surfaces that allow air to flow smoothly over them. The F-117A has angled surfaces. Pilots often have trouble keeping the F-117A straight and level during flight.

throttle — a control on an airplane that allows pilots to increase or decrease the plane's speed

The F-117A's cockpit has advanced equipment.

A computer connected to the pilot's controls helps make the F-117A fly like other planes. The computer makes small corrections for the pilot. Without the computer's help, the plane would fly out of control.

Protected Engines

Two jet engines power the F-117A. Each engine produces 10,600 pounds (4,808 kilograms) of thrust. This force pushes the plane through the air. To produce thrust, jet engines burn fuel. The burning fuel produces hot waste gases called exhaust. The plane moves forward as the exhaust rushes out of the engines at the plane's rear. The F-117A's engines give it a top speed of about 646 miles (1,040 kilometers) per hour.

Jet engines need a great deal of air to burn fuel. Large air intakes are located at the front of a jet engine. The air intakes show up on most radar systems. **Gratings** cover the F-117A's air intakes. These gratings are covered with RAM to hide the intakes from enemy radar.

grating — a grid of metal bars

F-117A Specifications

Function:	Stealth attack fighter
Manufacturer:	Lockheed Martin
Deployed:	1982
Length:	63 feet, 9 inches (19.4 meters)
Wingspan:	43 feet, 4 inches (13.2 meters)
Height:	12 feet, 9.5 inches (3.9 meters)
Weight:	52,500 pounds (23,625 kilograms)
Payload:	4,000 pounds (1,814 kilograms)
Engine:	Two General Electric F404 engines
Speed:	646 miles (1,040 kilometers) per hour
Range:	500 miles (805 kilometers); unlimited with in-flight refueling

The rear of each F-117A's engine has thin slots to protect the plane from heat-seeking missiles. A heat-seeking missile has a sensor in its nose. The sensor guides the missile toward heat from a plane's exhaust. The F-117A's engine slots help spread out the exhaust heat. The missile then cannot easily detect the heat.

cockpit

air intake gratings

facet

wing

The F-117A Nighthawk

tail

engine slots

Weapons and Tactics

Learn about

- F-117A bombs
- FLIR and DLIR systems
- Planning missions

The F-117A can carry two bombs inside its bomb bay. Enemy radar could detect the bombs if they were carried outside of the F-117A. The bomb bay's doors open to allow the pilot to drop the bombs.

Bombs

The F-117A carries laser-guided bombs (LGBs). The F-117A pilot aims a laser beam at a target. The bomb then follows the beam.

The F-117A often carries LGBs.

The Air Force has several 2,000-pound
(907-kilogram) LGBs. F-117A pilots often
use these bombs to destroy bridges, buildings,
and underground hideouts called bunkers.

The F-117A also can carry the GBU-27
LGB. The explosives inside the GBU-27
weigh 550 pounds (249 kilograms).
The bomb has a range of more than
10 miles (16 kilometers).

Target-Tracking Systems

F-117A pilots use two target-tracking systems. A Forward-Looking Infrared (FLIR) and a Downward-Looking Infrared (DLIR) system detect heat in objects. The head-up display (HUD) shows these objects. The systems can locate objects in the air and on the ground. They allow pilots to see targets up to 15 miles (24 kilometers) away.

Sensor pods hold the F-117A's FLIR and DLIR systems. The FLIR system is located below the pilot's cockpit. The DLIR system is below the nose of the aircraft. Pilots use the FLIR to help them fly the plane to the target. The DLIR system senses the target just before the plane flies over it.

Each sensor pod also contains a laser designator. Pilots use the designators to aim **laser beams** at targets after the target-tracking systems locate them.

laser beam — a narrow, intense beam of light

Combat Missions

Air Force officials carefully plan each F-117A mission. They gather as much information about a target as possible. The aircraft's automated mission-planning system processes the information. A computer creates a set of instructions for the F-117A. The computer uses the instructions to automatically fly the plane close to the target.

After the plane nears the target, the pilot makes sure the target is correct. The pilot then drops the bombs.

EDGE FACT

The F-117A has no gun for defense. Flying without a gun is one reason the plane flies only in the dark.

F-117As often fly in pairs during missions.

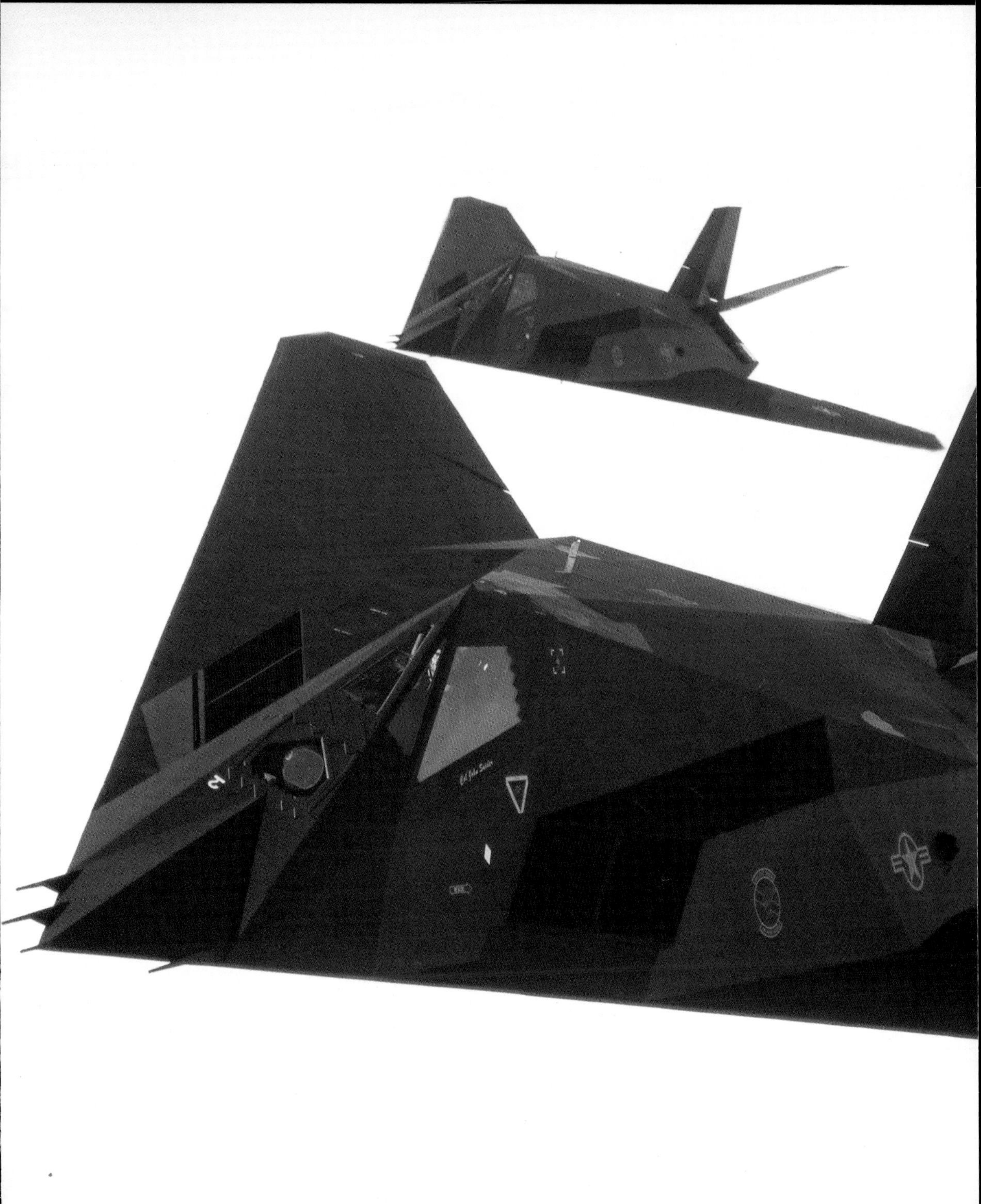

Serving the Military

Learn about
- Future usefulness
- New RAM
- JDAMs

The Air Force has used the F-117A for more than 20 years. The plane has flown on a variety of missions. During the Gulf War, F-117A pilots performed more than 1,250 missions. In 1999, the Air Force participated in Operation Allied Force in southern Europe. F-117A pilots successfully attacked highly defended targets during the operation.

Air Force officials do not plan to buy more F-117As. But they plan to keep the F-117A in service until at least 2018.

Improvements

The Air Force has improved the F-117A. In 1997, the Air Force began to equip F-117As with an improved navigation system called the RNIP-Plus. In the past, the navigational system sometimes caused the aircraft to stray from its flight path. The new system helps the aircraft stay on course.

Until the late 1990s, F-117A pilots could not communicate with anyone outside the aircraft during combat missions. Enemy forces can sometimes detect communication. F-117A pilots could not receive updated information after the mission started.

Today, F-117A pilots can receive information from spacecraft called satellites. This data can include weather information or a change in targets. Enemy forces cannot detect satellite messages.

In 2000, the Air Force began to replace the RAM on F-117As. In the past, F-117As had several different RAMs. The new RAM is a combination of several materials.

JDAMs

The Air Force plans to equip the F-117A with satellite-guided Joint Direct Attack Munitions (JDAMs) in the future. Poor weather conditions can cause LGBs to wander from their flight paths. Weather conditions do not affect satellite-guided weapons. The JDAM includes a kit that fits over the tail of an unguided bomb. The kit adds fins, a satellite receiver, and an electric motor to the bomb.

EDGE FACT

The F-117A Nighthawks often are the first planes sent out on important missions.

In the future, F-117As will be equipped with JDAMs.

The Air Force may stop flying the F-117A after 2018. Other militaries are developing improved radar systems. These systems may be able to detect the F-117A. Even if retired, the F-117A will always be an important plane in U.S. Air Force history.

GLOSSARY

altitude (AL-tuh-tood) — the height of an object above the ground

exhaust (eg-ZAWST) — heated air leaving a jet engine

facet (FA-suht) — a smooth, flat panel

grating (GRAY-ting) — a grid of metal bars

laser beam (LAY-zur BEEM) — a narrow, intense beam of light

radar (RAY-dar) — equipment that uses radio waves to locate and guide objects

sensor (SEN-sur) — an instrument that detects physical changes in the environment

throttle (THROT-uhl) — a control on an airplane that allows pilots to increase or decrease the plane's speed

thrust (THRUHST) — the force created by a jet engine; thrust pushes an airplane forward.

READ MORE

Hamilton, John. *The Air Force.* Defending the Nation. Edina, Minn.: Abdo, 2007.

Hopkins, Ellen. *U.S. Air Force Fighting Vehicles.* United States Armed Forces. Chicago: Heinemann Library, 2004.

Parks, Peggy J. *Fighter Pilot.* Exploring Careers. Detroit: Kidhaven Press, 2006.

INTERNET SITES

FactHound offers a safe, fun way to find Internet sites related to this book. All of the sites on FactHound have been researched by our staff.

Here's how:
1. Visit *www.facthound.com*
2. Choose your grade level.
3. Type in this book ID **1429613203** for age-appropriate sites. You may also browse subjects by clicking on letters, or by clicking on pictures and words.
4. Click on the **Fetch It** button.

FactHound will fetch the best sites for you!

INDEX